Bachpan And Baddua

Collection of Poems

Shifa Thakkar

BookLeaf Publishing
India | USA | UK

Made with ❤ on the BookLeaf Publishing Platform
www.bookleafpub.in
www.bookleafpub.com

Dedication

To the self
that I lost
to please the world.

Preface

Today, I am 31 years old, yet I feel lost. There are different sayings to 'start' whenever you are ready, but sadly, I never felt ready.

I don't remember at what age I asked my namesake father about turning into a girl with maybe magic. His reply, back then, felt soothing and encouraging.

I have been learning about my transness since childhood. From the beginning, I was told it is a shame to feel like a girl in a boy's body.

One day, I roughly remember our landowner telling the *Hijras* outside our door, who had come to ask for help and money to take me away with them.

My mother fought with her for 'degrading' me to them. Since that day, I felt anxious in front of my Hijra sisters, as if they would decode my sexuality. Hence, I never got to learn about my teenwood.

Everything post that incident shaped my life. To not see myself as a *Hijra*, I sought the path of seeing myself as a feminine gay individual. On dating/meeting apps, I told people I am *bottom* and played the role well.

But as my mind must have resisted the idea and feeling I outgrew everything. With the help of a psychiatrist and various examinations, I learned about my gender dysphoria. I learned there is a name for what I feel.

It took me since my puberty, 21 years to accept myself. Today, I can tell my friends, you and a few people, that I am a trans individual. And yet, I am following very measured steps to come out.

I am transitioning, but the method is a bit risky and irreversible. Trans individuals mostly start with Hormone Replacement Therapy as their first step to transition, and surgery, be it top or bottom, as last.

I do not know when you will get this book in your hand, but I hope that whenever it does, I will be in my whole body as a woman.

I am writing this book as a transition gift to myself. Here, through every page, I hope you will learn about me, my struggles, and the fight to come out of the closet.

Importantly, this book doesn't just talk about my trans identity, but a love that I have felt for people. I never got the chance to live a life with any of them, but somewhere through poetry, I am reliving the emotions I have felt for them and how loving them has shaped me. I hope you will relate to my unrequited emotions. I hope you can read the poetry through a trans gaze. I hope you will be able to understand, not just a social acceptance we trans are struggling with, but with the acceptance of our love for others.

Acceptance is kind, but the path to it can get rough due to the world. I hope this book becomes your friend and the help you have been looking for for a long time.

I want to share a heartfelt note to everyone: This book was not easy to shape. With care and understanding, I have arranged this collection of poetry. Before reading, I want to share a trigger warning. There are mentions of words like death, rape, suicide, and many more. So, please make your decision wisely. I do not wish to hamper anyone's mental health.

Read these poems with care and love. I wish you all the best.

Acknowledgements

How did this book become a reality? All thanks to Bookleaf Publishing House. Before I start ranting about how the Bookleaf platform has given me the vision and opportunity to come out of my closet to show my skills of articulation, I want to start with the gratitude I have for my mother.

As a child, I often blamed her for birthing me. I have learnt from my relatives that I was an 'accidental child'. I learnt that she didn't want me because she was scared she would give birth to a girl.

But as destiny must have tricked her, it gave her what she wanted: a boy with male genitalia. But neither did she have an idea nor I that I am beyond the genitals I was born with.

Hence, for whatever reason, she couldn't abort me, so I could get the chance at seeing this world. I thank her. But also, I would not have been bothered if she had succeeded in aborting me. She deserves happiness and not to be burdened with taking care of a baby she hadn't planned for.

I want to extend my thankfulness towards Ved, Kash, and Vish. These three are the reasons this book came into existence. My infatuation, obsession, and unrequited love made me write these words and give them a form of poetry.

My heartfelt gratitude to Maisha, they are the reason I could meet a beautiful person, Jai (Jia/Joya), their sibling. They both have encouraged me to improve my English and become confident in speaking it. Besides, they both have inspired me in many ways. I was able to understand my roots and caste.

Nilesh, my dearest friend, even if we are not on talking terms, I want to thank him. His love for reading books and constant curiosity have inspired me to love and read more books. He is the reason I have this book, which I am sure will become a part of someone's library and poetry collection.

I want to thank everyone on my WhatsApp list and people from the Instagram group. They all have endured my constant poem sharing for their feedback. Because of them, I was able to keep improving myself.

I want to thank my friend Ketan. He once complimented me on my birthday. He said that I write beautifully. He said, I should keep writing. And see, my friend, I have come very far. I have progressed.

Lastly, to my very first best friend, Shrikant. He is the reason I started writing. He is the reason I turned towards writing to express my emotion; he is the reason words came to me, and I was able to give them shape, a form, a body, and emotions.

And how could I forget my namesake father? He inspired me and has put a fire of hope in me in my early childhood to accept my sexuality.

I wish everyone to have a father like him. I wish things were progressive back then. I wish I were able to save him. I wish he were with me on this beautiful journey. But wherever he is, I hope he is safe, healthy, and happy. I love you, Pappa.

part one

the unborn child

1. Magic

When this body
was being made
in my mother's womb,
the cells I feel
fooled every part of her.

They asked for her chromosomes
but never used it.
They must have tricked her,
or were they aware of the death
that waited outside her womb for me?

They mismatched everything
because the men were ready
to eat me, snatch me, and throttle me.

Was I saved
by being born
into the wrong body?
Or was I put through this tragedy
because irrespectively
women live a hell?

I guess I will never find out.

But must I thank
the invisible power,
or naive science,
to give me a chance
to find myself?

Or allowing me to live a dual life
to hide from wolves?

2. Mirror

There is a story unrevealed,
in the emotions, the gestures he has lived;
the banarasi saree smells more of him,
struggling to live.

He would go to a friend of his,
his mother's lipstick he would steal,
and paint the reality concealed.
then an absoluteness he would feel.

Often, he would wear a ghagra,
and witness the transparency of his friend.
it would show the real him;
the one that needed no mending.

He would pretend sometimes the pain of bearing
a trauma of womanhood, his femininity
and then decorate them on his frugal, pretentious
masculinity.

There was a boy that wanted to live,
but his reflection in the mirror outlived him.

3. Consequences

My approach
at life,
to people,
is pessimistic.

I fall
before I begin
the jump.

I start
the sentence
with a touch of
end note to it.

Before I mould
any mud,
I begin
bickering
with nature
for being
too harsh.

I blame
the creator

for creating me,

I follow a ritual
to rampage
the very being of me,

I do everything
to become something
but I end up as nothing.

4. Valid

My grief is valid,
my pain is real.
I do not need to express it
or combat with it,
neither must I go battling it.
It is a part of me,
it is me.
It makes me,
it becomes me.

I, with my grief, become,
a source,
a channel,
a vessel--
to hold traumas of my bloodline,
to captive the wretchedness within
and grow with it,
or grow out of it.

I am not obliged to anyone
to listen to their toxic positivity.
I am a body, a home,
I have emotions
and I will want to grief.

I can draw the curtains of misery
and weep behind the darkness
about losing someone
who still lives.

I am not a machine.
I am a human; it is my nature to be sad.
No self-help book should tell me otherwise,
no speaker on the podium gets the right
to devalue my hurting and to say to me it is just a phase.

I know it could be a phase
but I still want this phase to be part of me
to feel human, to understand the vulnerability
and to not go insane.

I am the bones of breakdowns.
I am the skin of sorrows.
I am the eyes of agony.
I am the teeth of tragedy.
I am hands of hurting.
I am the legs of lament.
I am the hunger humiliated.
I am the fingers of fragility.
I am the toes to tear apart.
I am a human, and I will perish.

There is no sense in pretense
or in hollow cheer-ups and fake smiles.
If I am sad,
it will be on my face
grieving with me.

Because, I am the garth of glumness.

5. Identity

People presume playing
is a part of children's activity,

I do not recall
when I started this game.
I am playing, it's been years.

I have played a homosexual,
I have played many alphabets.

(I should stop now.)

But what do I see myself as?
I do not want to feel pride at
calling myself human.

It is the default,
I am more than
these bones that hold me,
I am more than the words I speak.

I am a hub of emotions,
I played pretend
but now I want to pass,

I want to preserve
and breathe my identity.

I want the world to know me for me,
I am a girl trapped
not just in a man's body,
I am a soul trapped under
the pressure of society.

I am a woman.
I am making myself from scratch,
I am picking every jewel
this world made me throw
in fear of being caught.

I am relentless.
I will stop only when
I start breathing myself again.

6. Rebirth

I am unable to write poetry tonight.

My mind is scattered.
There is an urgency
in my actions.

I am in a hurry.

I have nowhere to reach
but there is an excitement.

Oct 9th, 2025
and a new life:
from my self that was stolen,
hidden from the world,
covered up in lies.

I will live, hopefully,
after all those deaths
that I mourned
to become myself.

7. Remembrance

The first conversation
from my memory
of wanting to be a girl
was with my father.

He spoke about life
as if I was accustomed
with the language.
He soothed me,
said, I am, what I feel.

I said less
but begged more
for the word of affirmation,
naive, I was,
but my desires
were mature.

I asked,
what does it take
to be a girl,
a miracle, he said,
a prayer, he suggested,

but he forgot to add
'a will and self-acceptance'

part two

loveless child

1. Poetry

How do I define
this wretched world
that is woven
within this body?

I know not
when I have
become this.

I do not recall
learning
to pour pessimism
in my poetry

Anger, anguish, alien emotions
I remember housing them,
I recall being raped
before knowing love,

I know not
love among siblings,
I have felt fights,
punches and abuse
from my loved ones.

Maybe the love
I was told about
was the only love
my elders knew?

Maybe love is abusive?

How else can we define it:
if not, it to be the death of us?

2. Colourblind

In this colours splattered galaxy--
symbolising the various forms of love,
we are lost within,
colorblind to each other.

3. Thin Layers

In between death
and my struggle to breathe
it seems easy to choose to sleep,

I don't want
to fight the waves
that rage inside my chest
I just want to rest.

Maybe on the other side
there is serenity
or a new death,

Nonetheless
I need death.
I need rest.

4. Chaos

It's okay
to breathe less,
or breathe fast,
or breathe with,
a shiver down the spine.

It's okay
to think less,
or think more,
or think nothing.

It's okay
to lose yourself,
to want to lose yourself,
to choose to lose yourself
to find your new again.

World tells us
water mould with shapes,
but it's okay if water waves,
or there is a whirl in it.

We learn to think straight,
but it is okay if we forget

how to think,
or where to begin thinking.

World will want us to stay,
but it is okay if we lose ourselves
in the embrace of our feelings,
in the grip of loved ones,
in the thoughts of friends,
or over just a cup of chai.

Permanency is an illusion,
nothing is forever!
why pledge something
when there is an end to everything?

5. Fire

I wish I could cry
and let out this anger.

I want this
lava to out
and burn the forest,
all the gardens,
the heavens
I have fantasied
for you, with you.

I wish everything to end
but I am not ready
to be charred in the heat.

6. Sacrifice

I couldn't share the love,
But I know how it feels
when it is shared.

I wait for a man
to get engulfed in his smell
and a strong embrace,

My body is too soft to hold,
I want him to hug me tight
and make me believe
I won't be left alone.

He will be there to touch me
and console me when upset,
he will dare to lift my face
and ask me to look into
his mesmerizing eyes,

He will make me believe
with his smile and shiny eyes,

and I will,
like a life, like a breath

will believe him.

Even if at the end
death takes me away,
if that is the price I have to pay,
I am ready for it.

I can lose my breath
for my man's love for me.

7. What does Depression Look Like?

It looks like me, a healthy skeleton.
I can say I have a friend, eventually
who has planned to stick around.

This time I am not worried
of being left alone.
With my dearest friend,
I always feel the need to be alone.

I spend most of my time with Depression
I cook, clean, eat, and bathe
or I do nothing.

Sometimes, I attend meetings,
or walk through the garden
in search of nothing,
I don't brag about my friend
I enjoy the part where I can have a secret friend.

When people come to meet me
I try to hide it.
I imitate the fake smiling people give,
I chirp as if I have the most melodious voice,

I eat like a buffalo and drink like a horse.

I participate in games with them.
I know I am good at ditching people,
obscuring my reality,
I learned these tactics in my childhood.
It was a gift from my mother.

I look forward to
drowning evenings,
everything silent
like my mind,
everything stopped
like my thoughts,
everything dead,
like me.

I have a friend I never thought to have
and I don't know how not to have it.

8. Home

I do not have
a place or a person
to call it home

I do not have
courage to find one

All I can do
is live in a fantasy land
and make it
my own safe space

It may not be
an ideal fit for
a human soul

but I trap myself
in that world anyways.

9. Loneliness

I have become
an empty vessel

no amount of
emotions now
can fill my void

I am lost
like I have
thousands of time

I still can't
find me

I don't know
how to find me

I don't know
how to fill me
with love

all that reverberates
in this shallowness
is my loneliness

10. Fragrance

I don't know
how does a man's face smell
when he comes close
to your lips to kiss you.

Many men have painted
their yearning on my lips,
but never could I smell
any love whiffing out of their mouth
or their body.

All I could smell was
a distinct odor
which I didn't want to home
or get hella crazy for!

I crave though
like a starved soul,
for a body to home me
and kiss me,

for eternity.

11. Closer

Sun-sets, and so does my heart,
it falls under the rubble
of my undefined misery.

I lay beneath the moonless sky
and think of ways
to get lost in the darkness.

I can't, I tell myself
I should not,
I can't escape,
I don't want to be
remembered as a coward.

But my helplessness
makes me do things
which doesn't kill me
but takes me to my death
one step closer.

12. Discomfort

I do not savour self-love
but dislike for me.

Is it hate
or discomfort?
Or restlessness with
my being?

I do not know.

All I know is
I want to scrape this skin,
take a new form,
become a new being,
leave my old self behind
and remember what I should be,

But have kept it hidden
for the sake of the world.

13. Goodbye

I knew the depth of the ocean
but I chose to drown in it anyway.

I was aware I would struggle to breathe
but I jumped into the waters with the risk.

No, I wasn't told if I would die,
I thought I would learn to
survive in the alien environment.

But now I understand,
there is no going back!
Except giving in
and allowing the waves
to take me with them.

14. Survival

Love so pure,
I assume
it doesn't exist.

I wait for it, anyway,
as if it will show up
at my empty door.

I will survive,
live through its absence,
breathe, instead of dying.

I won't be homesick,
alone, or devastated.

But love so pure
is havoc,
don't they say?

I may get lost in its storm
and wither at its hand,
yet flourish at the end.

Love so pure is a poison,

I may not want to die,
but I fear I will drink it anyway.

Because love,
in any means,
is a way of living.

15. The Coward

Dying must not be easy
or else
I would have laid
at the crest of the ocean,
or beneath the sand,
or would have lost
into thin air.

I am a coward.
I don't dare to harm myself,
I am afraid I will fail
like my life has failed me.

I don't want to leave
but my emotions have
left my body,

I don't know
how long
I can carry this skeleton.

But as long as
I am alive,
I know,

I am aware,
I will have to
keep dying every day
to die eventually one day.

16. A Gift

Unnerving palpilations
was a gift,
It was a gift
from me for me.

I am unsure
when I received it,
I don't remember
the celebration
when I planned to gift it to me,

But I feel it,
it's my home
every evening.

I slip into the nothingness
like I have been there before,
long before I learned about feelings,
maybe it was in my mother's womb?

I stay restless
until sleep comes to me,
and I hope
when I go to bed

this night will be the last one,

But when I wake up
I get up dead.

I had to cherish my gift,
Nonetheless.

17. Nuclei

I'm told that my words bleed pessimism—
But how should I explain to them
That it was the fodder I was fed with

And that I want to still
Keep feeding on it?

I want to write about love
And no one losing it
No one wilting at the longings—

But I become speechless
I lose my vocabulary
I remember my anxiety
The palpitations in my heart—

I go numb from the happiness of it.
I'm alive because I live deaths.

18. The End

I'm dead
a stone-like,
A man from the desert
Or a desert itself,

Shiny showers are far gone
buds have forgotten budding,
roads now grow thorns,

The man who will walk into me
the one who will be close
the man who will love me
will be shattered into pieces
because the pain is me,
because the destruction is me,
because the havoc is me,
because the end is me,
because the dead is me.

19. Window

When the mason had asked me the size of the window
I would like to have for my room
I said huge enough to throw out my rage through it,

To the east? He then asked.
no, cut it out where the sun dies.
I spat at him.

I sit by it now; no, I am not angry,
I am anxious; I don't know how to scrape this feeling off,
the taste of it feels homely
I have lived with it since I learned emotion.

The light arrives and departs, but the darkness stays,
I hear the sound of everything but me,
my mind seems to have lost its voice.

The dust that accumulates at the windowsill and on
metal--
I sketch memoirs of my sadness on them.
it doesn't ask me if I have a story to tell
but listens when I speak my silence to it.

There is, behind this transition, a world I know of

which separates me from reality
and there is a world that rests unrecognized
inside me

But it is defined by a window.

20. Stake

I am a fool,
I give away
myself,
my self-respect,
my identity,
my honour.

To the one
who is not
a man of words
or worth.

To allow him
to degrade
and disregard me
enough
Until I kill myself.

What I see
in these men
or what I ignore
so strongly
about me

That before they fail me at life
I drop down dead.

21. Pledge

People burn me,
they scrape
my flesh
through
until my naked bone
cracks open
and is visible
for them to
nail their obscenity
on me.

Now, do I
allow them
to put me on fire
and play with my flesh?

I think I do;
how is it justified, then?
my body belongs to me
but my mind
is manipulated by people.

I am not my own,
I am pledged to people.

22. Philanthropy

I play on the internet
battleground
with words of plea,

society mocks me
with papers,
metal made coins:
to degrade my identity

To begin with-
I have none,
I have become
nameless glorified beggar!

I beg to live,
they charity
to keep me alive.

I suffer
to suffice,
their hunger for
namesake philanthropy.

23. Manifestation of Love

Some sing
their heart to people,

some make
brushes dance,

some make
words weep on paper,

some move
their fingers,
and change
the rhythm of the world.

and some on a burning flame
create lips-smacking love
for their beloved.

But I create love
At your mere existence.

24. Second Chance

I am sad
I can say,
but I don't know
who holds the reins
to my sadness.

I only know
that I wanted
to be nurtured
a bit more from yesterday,

a bit more, I felt,
I must be told
I am important
again,

how frugal
my flowers are,
I lose my own
fragrance,
in the play
to please
alien buds.

I must smell
ill or less tempting,
for the bees too
turn away

I feel no hurt
when I am not loved,
I am hurt
when I am not the one
receiving love.

I feel like
an empty shell
that has distanced
from the shore,
from the snail,
from a life,
that once birthed
and breathed
on its inside.

I may need a second life
to give love a second chance
to choose me first
the next time.

24. Pretense

Be the broken piece
at heart and soul.

I don't fancy
the wholesome.

How will I
put perfection
before the world

When I have
only known
the incompleteness
and void.

part three

unrequited love

1. Chance

I
do not
want to give you
a chance
in my poetry

Yet
you live in my every word.

2. Madness

I am consumed
I overthink you,
My world ends
at the periphery
of your body.

I wave like water
between depression
and madness,
I want to swim
on your skin

but I drown
in your hollowness.

3. Suffering

I could never be me
I think of you and become you, for you.

I see you, I think of myself to be stronger,
I lie beautifully.

I hope life will become easy for me,
But then I call you and make everything not matter

I tell myself I will move on,
And I move away from me.

I want to not hang in your thoughts,
About situations where you calm me
I want to become the ocean by myself.

I ask for sleep to come to me
after everything that has happened,

But anger enters my body
the minute I hear your voice
muttering her name.

Sleeplessness would have been fun,
But I devour the habit of suffering.

4. Remembrance II

I want to leave
I'm tired of games, you.
I want to move somewhere
Maybe away from you?
No.

I'm unable to.
I can't go!
I want you to stop me—
Maybe hold me close?

Tell me you are not afraid?
Do things what lovers do?
Change the world?
Or let's change it together?

Fight for me!
Scream, forget what silence means,
Tell the world that I'm your world!

Make the world believe we are part of this world.

If not, let me breathe last,
Let me see you at last,

Be my last.

When this air gets out of me,
Maybe breathe me in for the last time
As a remembrance.

5. Control

Last night
I lost control,
I pinged you
and it pierced
right through my heart.

I forget reaching you
should be unreachable.

I do the unknown.
I play the game
Of hide and seek

And forget
I will never be sought.

6. Separation

I wish
I hadn't allowed you
on my land of love.

You pretended to plant
seeds of affection
but they flourished
into a brutal presentation.

I have become the cloud,
I rain on every terrain,
I scrape my skin now
with tears of separation.

7. Grief

You are dead
but you killed me
in the process,

I lived because
you breathed.

Now that your breath
has become sour
I have become bitter.

I am lost
I am in pain
I am dying.

Your every step
away from me
takes a part of my body
and hammer it
with the weight of grief
of your death.

8. Parting Gift

I have cried
for a single gift
from you.

A kiss,
an embrace,
or maybe
just a touch-
a handshake?

What you gave me
I don't deserve.

I deserve life
but you killed me
every time I walked
towards you.

You chose to
bury me with your lies.
cover me up
with the pretence.

I lay here

with a hope,
that you will
dig this grave
one day, in pity,

And offer me love
as my parting gift.

9. Tinder Date

Words we have shared
Words we have become.
We don't know
What we will be called
But we know we will be known.

Friends from strangers,
Lovers in the making?

Whatever we would be
It won't be meaningless.
Whatever we should be
We will be.

One for another
Or for eachother.

10. Flip

Things have changed
Since you happened

There is comfort,
But a hesitation in expression
There is my voice,
But full of questions.

There is you
Full of her,
And there is me,
All about you.

11. Empty

You leave,
I become the void,
it sets in,

You are nowhere around,
I battle the emptiness alone.

I know I can lift the darkness
with or without you.

But I disregard my presence,
I allow the absence
to overpower me.

I allow your entireness
to empty me.

12. Wait

My hands are trembling
My fingers itch to dial you
I do not buy heart know your number
But the saved figures
can help me rest my soul in peace

Instead of calling you
I imagine things,
I'm good at them
I'm thinking you are busy surfing
Through your phone?
Maybe too busy on Facebook
To recall, we are not friends there!

Maybe you are tired
With your all day work,
You want rest, sleep and food
And you are waiting for them eagerly.

Or maybe you are full,
Full of stomach and happiness
And for the call
You would get at midnight.

I should not tarnish that
I should not destroy myself over you
And your assumed happiness
I must remain silent
Until my silence makes
The unbearable noise in your ears.

13. End

What did you give me
if not pain,
paralyzing trauma?

What did I do
to deserve this?
my desires to wish you
resulted in death sentence,
silence and suppression

I am angry
I want things to end
but I wish it starts with your end.

14. Missing Piece

I'm going back,
walking backwards,
towards the past
in the dark,
to reach you
again.

I wished at first
you will be mine,
now I wish-
at least at last
you will want
to be mine.

Not because I waited,
but you finally found
the missing piece
for your misery
to vanish.

15. A New Chapter

A mystery,
a memory,
a fling
you have become

I don't recall the hurt
nor how unpleasant
our first kiss was.

There is an image,
it is blurring
everyday since
I have left you.

The patches of wound
from your pain
has healed,
I am no hollow
to make a jarring sound.

I have become
full of myself
and less of you,

We have come to an end,
I have started myself
from the beginning.

16. Honey Words

Your opinion arouses me more
than your curved body,

Dare you speak to me,
and I am awake, fresh,
ready to immerse
to your honey words.

17. Wrong Education Of Love

I am taught otherwise.

I was told
to be in love
is to have
infatuation, obsessions.

The understanding of love is-
it is neither on the face
or in their pants
but in communication.

No one said that the faces
I will be attracted to the most
will not decide my life,
or my existence.

The places I will go to
could bring new,
fresh love for me,

the one I leave behind
will not become my past

but more likely a part of me.

No one said
the person I will feel love for
may not feel the same,
even if I cross oceans
or boundaries of comfort.

The love I will receive will be the love
that wants to be with me
and not because I demand it!

The love that doesn't want to stay
I will have to learn
to let it go
and not make it feel caged
or manipulate it for personal ego.

My beloved could die before me,
and sadly, I would lose love,
but the death of one partner
will not be the ending of my living
I could be living and loving
one or many.

My love could be
more than just a feeling,

less physical, less about souls!

I am taught otherwise,

I am channelled to see anger
as a way of returning love.
their passive behaviour
a call to chase the lost love,

I wish I was told
that the love is not about
having but feeling-
in depths like an ocean
and vast as the azure sky.

18. Doomsday

At the edge of the earth, there lies
its end–
the end of humanity, of living beings.

There is no place except you
worth living for.
Nothing is worth fighting for.

It's our togetherness
which gives me the strength
to keep us whole.

The happiness, the sorrows–
the days, months, eternity
revolve around you.

But there is an end in sight–
things will fall apart.
they will come to a finish.
with you, or without me.

19. Beyond the Obvious

Who are you
when the sun
hides itself
behind this
pearly clouds,

tell him
to meet me
I want to
see that *'you.'*

The real, the fragile,
or the strongest
as the storms!

Postface

Now that you have completed reading the collection of poems, take a breath. Sit with yourself and close your eyes. Let everything that you have read make sense to you and help you accept every emotion that resonated with you from this book.

You have come this far; I am proud of you. Pat yourself on your back, you dived in the ocean of emotions and have swum out from the land of your comfort. You have accepted yourself. You have accepted that you have a feeling, and it is okay to feel, so stay in touch with them.

When you close this book, please do not put it on the shelf, pass it on, gift it, or lend it to your friend.

Let my words reach more people. Let love become the language of living.

With love,
Shifa

About the Author

Shifa (chosen name), Shailesh (birth name), is a Dalit Transqueer individual from Navi Mumbai. Shifa loved writing since she completed her Secondary Section School.

From a very early childhood, she had to go out for work. Being a part of a family where the father was an addict and the mother with social anxiety, she couldn't get far with her life financially and socially.

Her trans identity, her femininity, made things worse for her. On one hand, she had to accept herself, and on the other, her fate and future, which depended on earning and surviving daily.

Her struggles have brought her here today. She is among people through the medium of this book. She hopes to reach into the hearts of many.

Learn more about her through Instagram and other social media platforms. To reach out to her, do send an email to jsjolly2501@gmail.com

www.ingramcontent.com/pod-product-compliance
Lightning Source LLC
LaVergne TN
LVHW022015200926
848481LV00007B/2409
* 9 7 9 8 9 0 0 8 1 5 0 5 3 *